Apulia

History Art Landscape

by Lorenzo Capone

Translated by Letizia Ferrari

Capone Editore

Capone Editore

via prov.le Lecce-Cavallino, Km 1,250
Tel. 0832.612618 / 0832.611877 (fax)
Mail to: info@caponeditore.it
on line: www.caponeditore.it

ISBN 88-8349-049-5

Le foto appartengono all'archivio della Casa Editrice
Altre referenze fotografiche:
Pierluigi Bolognini pagine 37 (destra), 49 (sotto), 50 (sotto), 91;
Ornella Cucci 7 (sotto); Claudio Grenzi 41 (sotto), 48 (sotto);
Claudio Longo 49 (sopra), 50 (sopra)

© Copyright 2003 - Capone Editore

Stampa: Stampa: Tiemme Ind. Grafica s.r.l. - Manduria (Ta)
Lastre digitali: DigitEdit s.r.l. - Manduria (Ta)

«... it is an inventory which is lacking in soòething like any inventory: omissions and gaps cathc one's eye».

Guido Piovene

This statement suits me.

Lorenzo Capone

Meeting point of civilisations

All surrounded with the sea

Apulia is the only region to have so much sea. There are eighty hundred kilometres of coast surrounding it from the border with Molise, between Campomarino and the mouth of the Fortore, on the Adriatic sea, to the mouth of the Bradano, near Metaponto, on the Ionian sea.

The history of Apulia has developed along this coastline, in some parts high and steep to the sea (the Gargano and the Salento from Otranto to Santa Maria di Leuca), in some others low and sandy, with very long beaches which are crowded with millions of tourists. The first inhabitants of the region coming from Illyria, someti-

Wonderful Apulia
by Lino Patruno

I do not know whether Apulia is a wonderful land for its "windows" open to the sun, for its fall of light or for the dazzling sea surrounding it. I do not know whether it is wonderful for its dazzling white houses and the so called washed "chianche" or for its bread, for its oil like mother milk, for its secret orchids, or for its strange languages of the world. I do not know whether Apulia is wonderful for its local dance (pizzica pizzica) or for its thorny sea-urchins, for its underground churches, for its fires and very small houses or perhaps because it is "stony" and "dry", or for its castles recalling Merlin the Wizard or for the high cathedrals, its uses and customs or for its civilizations and cultures. I do not know whether Apulia is wonderful for its golden fields of wheat, red poppies, golden beaches, green olive-trees or white salt, for the sound of its night birds and

its sky or for the calm of the surf in the sunshine.

I do not know whether Apulia is wonderful for its grottoes "sculpted" by the water, for its windy areas, for the geraniums on small balconies, for some sheep-like villages, for the old farmhouses, for its ancient history, for the jewels of its women seeming the Madonna, for its healing and revengeful saints or for its San Father Pio.

I do not know whether Apulia is wonderful for its Eastern and Western influences or for its Eastern laziness and Western concreteness, for its simple but rich dishes, for its typical streets or for its boats among the rocks, for its wine as black as ink, for the dairy products or for the dewy gardens.

I only know that Apulia is wonderful even if I cannot explain for what exact reason.

Lino Patruno - Ornella Cucci, *Puglia meravigliosa*, Capone Editore 2001

Santa Maria di Leuca, villa Mellacqua

mes for choice or by chance, landed along this coastline; then arrived the Greeks, fleeting from the mother country or in search of a new land; here sacked the pirates dominating the Mediterranean – the fiercest of whom were those headed by Ariademo Barbarossa, lord of Algeri and Tunisi, in the first decades of the 16th century-; here the Sublime Door lorded it occupying Otranto in 1480, although for short time, therefore along these coasts many people have met and clashed for many years. Apulia is still today the border region which harbours thousands of refugees coming, as in the past, from the East, also thanks to its position in the heart of the Mediterranean.

Reaching this land from north, as soon as we go down southwards from Tavoliere to the land of Bari first and Salento later, we can seem to touch the scent and taste of the East. They alternate with a whole world made up of the landscape, architecture, customs, music, gastronomy which is often the East. "Apulia – Guido Piovene writes in his Viaggio in Italia – is the region where we can more perceive the East".

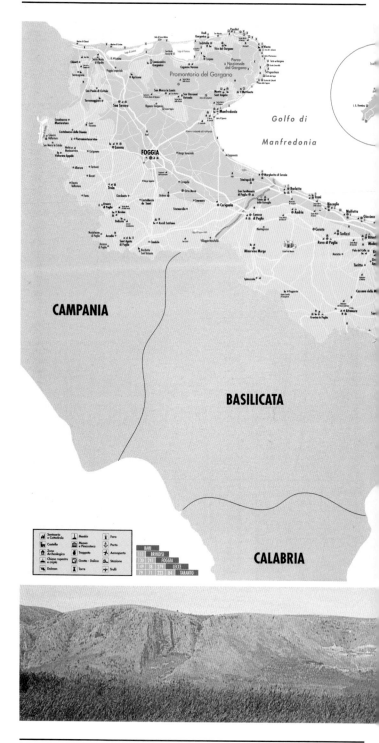

M A R

A D R I A T I C O

Golfo di

Taranto

Canale d'otranto

The Cathedrals

Troia, rosette on the front of the Cathedral

Apulia is not only this, it is also the West with its great Cathedrals which, for the local architectural features, have given way to the Apulian Romanesque style.

Going down from north southwards we find in the area of Foggia, the Cathedral of **Bovino**, devoted to Our Lady, one of the most ancient examples of Apulian Romanesque style. It has one nave and two aisles, an only apse, with columns and capitals and the front often rebuilt owing to the continuous destructions and reconstructions suffered by the town.

In the area of Capitanata we can find **Troia**'s Cathedral, devoted to Our Lady too, with bronze doors moulded by Oderisio from Benevento and with the great eleven-ray crenellated rosette.

In the province of Bari, **Trani**, there is the Cathedral devoted to San Nicola Pellegrino, with its front in local white marble from which

Trani, the front of the Cathedral

"appear" few figures of animals, with a bronze door by Barisano from Trani, with the 12th century bell-tower by *Nicolaus Sacerdos e Protomagister*, a significant emblem of Romanesque style among the most important ones in Italy (it was built on the church devoted to Santa Maria della Scala, the latter built on the hypogeum of San Leucio).

We also find **Ruvo**'s Cathedral whose front has side sloping pitches making it seem high and imposing (it was built, according to actual excavations, on a pagan temple). At **Altamura** the Cathedral, ordered to be built by Frederick II, has the front dominated by two bell-towers and the portal, richly decorated, has in the gable the Virgin on the throne. **Bitonto**'s Cathedral, devoted to San Valentino, which

Bari, the front of the Basilica of San Nicola.
On next page: Otranto

"seems to be a reduction in scale - Pina Belli d'Elia declares - of San Nicola, without the fascinating irregularities of that work", shows the ambo made by *Nicolaus Sacerdos*, representing a series of Swabian characters .In **Bari** we find the imposing Basilica of San Nicola which for the plan and the front, although its simple general plan, with windows with one and two lights giving a sense of lightness, has been an example for many buildings throughout the years. The Cathedral devoted to San Sabino, less known but equally important, instead, has a less austere front.

Going down southwards we find **Rutigliano**'s Cathedral, devoted to Santa Maria della Colonna and **Conversano**'s Cathedral with a lion bearing each columns and guarding the entrance-door. In **Taranto**'s Cathedral whose front was redone in the

18th century, besides admiring the magnificent wooden ceiling we must visit the Baroque chapel of San Cataldo, patron of the town, with its polychrome marbles (Gustavo Meyer-Graz, a German traveller, after visiting Taranto at the end of 19th century, defined "horrible" this superabundance of Baroque decorations), but also the crypt with some Byzantine frescoes. In the province of Lecce stands out **Otranto**'s Cathedral, with Latin cross, one nave and two aisles, with its essential front where a big rosette "dominates". Inside we can notice the magnificent floor-mosaic, recently restored, made by a monk, Pantaleone representing the tree of life. We must visit the Martyrs' Chapel hosting the relics of Otranto people beheaded on the nearby Minerva's hill in 1480 as well as the splendid crypt where many marble columns with various capitals and colours separate the inner rooms and support the vault.

They are all are works realised between the 12th and 13th centuries, thanks to the skills of great architects who used the tough local stone. They are buildings which have survived throughout the centuries, sometimes built in honour of Eastern saints like Bari's church devoted to San Nicola, a bishop from Mira, a small Turkish town of Licia near today's Turkey , from where, mariners from Bari, in 1087 stole the relics of the Saint.

From later period is Lucera's Cathedral, "the first Apulian building which can be considered –d'Elia writes- really Gothic, an Italian

Gothic style though". It has one nave and two aisles and a Latin cross, devoted to Our Lady, ordered to be built by Carlo d'Angiò in the 14th century on a mosque razed to the ground. Instead, **Canosa**'s Cathedral is from earlier time, probably dating back to the 11th century as some architectural remains bear witness to and built on San Sabino's tomb, as somebody says. Beside it we find the tomb of Boemondo (the hero of the first crusade, dead in 1111), square with a small vault and Eastern details.

Of the original building, originating from the 7th century construction, *Acceptus*'s pulpit and the bishop's throne by Romualdo have been preserved, the latter supported by two elephants while on the frontal slab we find

The Cathedral of Lucera.
On next page: Galatina, Santa Caterina d'Alessandria

two small sculptured eagles. **Cerignola**'s Cathedral has the same dome as Santa Maria del Fiore's in Firenze.

Santa Caterina d'Alessandria, at Galatina, remains an example of Gothic architecture: it was built in the first decades of 1300 by the powerful Orsini del Balzo family and given as a gift to the Franciscans.

The pictorial decoration is very rich: the frescoes, mostly in good conditions, decorate the nave, the presbytery and even others, from different periods, on the aisles. **Ostuni**'s Cathedral, built about the half of the 15th century, has an uneven front with curves and reverse curves, divided into three parts by two pilaster strips, with three ogival arched portals and an imposing central twenty-four ray rosette which is not comparable with others from Apulian churches. We can find again the front of Ostuni at Laterza, Manduria, Maruggio, etc. A real architectural jewel is San Giovanni al Sepolcro in Brindisi, dating back to the 11th century, one of the best example of Norman architecture. But any part of the region has its own church which has marked the history, from the 12th century Cathedral of **Mottola**, restored three centuries later, to the churches on the outskirts such as: Santa Maria Maggiore and San Leonardo at **Siponto**; from the convent of Santa Maria dell'Isola, at

Ostuni, the front of the Cathedral.
On next page: Siponto, Santa Maria Maggiore
and, *below*, Santa Maria a Cerrate

Conversano, with the splendid sepulchre of Giulio Antonio Acquaviva and the ogival arched cloister, to Sant'Apollinare at **Rutigliano**, to the small welcoming church of Santa Maria di Barsento at **Noci**, in the homonymous farmhouse, dating back to the 6th century, one of the first best preserved Apulian churches, to the Byzantine church of San Bartolomeo di Padula, built in the 11th century, six kilometres far from Castellana Grottoes, to the small Romanesque church of the Sanctuary of Madonna de Bernis o d'Ibernia, outside Cisternino, dating back to the 12th century, with a rosette, a sail-shaped bell-tower, three simple portals corresponding to

the aisles. The Romanesque church of Santa Maria di Cerrate, dating back to the 12th century, is very elegant, it is in the middle of an interesting abbatial building in the land of **Squinzano**: the one-nave and two-aisle church, with an interesting portal, has on left a wide and beautiful loggia facing the rooms intended for monks, under which an olive-mill is being restored. We must notice the small well in front of the loggia and we must also visit the Museum of Salento Popular Arts and Traditions.

The Castles

Besides the cathedrals Apulia boasts many civil and military buildings that are imposing and magnificent too such as: the castles, seats of power but also places for defence, meeting and clash, hunting and entertainment as well as the defence and watch towers which, especially between the 15th and 16th centuries, sprang up like mushrooms along the whole coastline of South and Apulia in particular, in order to prevent the continuous sudden assaults on the part of the pirates but also the attacks from the Ottoman fleet aiming at extending their own borders towards the West.

Castel del Monte is certainly the most original castle of its kind and not only in Italy.

It was ordered to be built

On this page and on previous one: Castel del Monte

in the first half of the 13th century by Frederick II who is supposed to have never visited it and we do not know yet what it was destined for in the past: it might have been a hunting residence or a defence building. Surely the octagonal structure dominates the whole northern Apulia: from the castle, the eyes rove over the Gulf of Manfredonia and the southern Gargano, and the building can be seen from afar. It is an architectural *unicum*. As Frederick and his court were interested in esoteric doctrines the building has a mysterious aspect which many to-

Castel del Monte
It is described by two travellers:
Janet Ross and Ferdinand Gregorovius

Reaching Apulia, like other regions in the south of Naples meant till after the unity of Italy venturing on a trip up an unknown continent for the difficulties of communications, for the lack of services but especially for the bands of the brigands who raged along the roads.

Going through the gorges of Bovino meant committing one's soul to God and many travellers, before leaving, used to make their will.

Nevertheless, the spirit of adventure which during the centuries has induced many foreign travellers to go to Apulia and follow the traces of what had remained of the Magno-Greek ancient times or to search for the Frederick age's findings has left significant marks in the region. Castel del Monte was an obliged halt for its magnificence.

Janet Ross, *La Puglia nell'Otocento*, Capone Editore, 1997
Ferdinand Gregorovius, *In Puglia*, Capone Editore, 2002

Janet Ross, a strange English traveller, reached Apulia at the end of 19th century and went to Castel del Monte. "After leaving the coach in an isolated farmhouse we began to go up the bare hill, under a scorching sun; then we realised that what had seemed to us a round tower was, instead, a perfect octagonal structure with a tower on each side and each tower had an octagonal shape… Between one tower and another there is an elegant Gothic window separated by a small rosy marble column and supported with a rosette. The window dominating the central door is bigger than thr others and it is adorned with small columns and, above, with beautiful transennae…

…The main door, in the middle of two towers, is in rosy marble and faces the sea from the eastern part; its Gothic arch is supported with two great lions which, similar to guardians, are located on two capitals of the columns flanking the splendid door. The whole is really wonderful for the fusion of Gothic and Classical styles, of Renaissance and ancient arts and it shows a splendid effect of architectural harmony and, at the same time, an elegant and austere aspect".

Ferdinand Gregorovius, a famous German historian who had come to Apulia more times in the second half of the 19th century so described Castel del Monte: "Riding towards the castle is my best record of my trips. We were seven. The local horses we rode on were big and strong. The men in our company were vigorous and strong, they had armed themselves with double-garrelled guns and they had taken the pistols too. The Murgia, like the Sila in Calabria, has never been a sure place...

It is a pleasure to ride through miles of waste and solitary country, to breathe the balmy air in May, all impregnated with the scent of many flowers and to see afar the dazzling blue sea.

As we went on riding along the green hills the castle with its yellowed walls began to appear...we kept astonished to find the superb castle in better conditions than we expected to. Inside it is in ruins and even outside it is spoiled...

If we see it in the whole it seems a marble structure instead of a fortress...Its forms are simply classic and you keep astonished to see them and you can realise the architecture during Hohenstaufen family's times...You do not find the typical heavy Medieval castle. The Gothic features appear more purified ...Doors and windows are Gothic or half-Gothic but the ogival arches, all adorned together with cornices, pediments, pillars and columns recall the ancient and classical form...

It is not easy to find or imagine a similar architectural building almost representing perfect mathematical rules..."

The castle of Trani and, below, that of Manfredonia.
On next page: the castle of Barletta

day's scholars from all over the world have been studying.

Apulia has many castles in the inland and especially in the coastal towns where they are much more imposing. In the area of Foggia we find **Vieste**'s castle, built thanks to Frederick II in 1240 and restored in the 16th century and another at **Manfredonia**, built by Manfred and completed under the reign of d'Angiò family. Going down southwards, in the province of Bari, **Barlet-ta**'s castle, begun to be built during Norman period, communicates with the sea and it is sur-

The castle of Bari.
On next page: the walls of Otranto (*above*) and the castle of Gallipoli

rounded with a wide moat.

Trani's castle, instead, smaller than Bari's, dates back to Frederick age but later redone by the Angevins. **Bari**'s castle, from Frederick time too, has hosted the duchess Isabella d'Aragona's

and Bona Sforza's (once queen of Poland) courts.

In the south-east of the area of Bari we find **Mola**'s castle, built in the second half of 13th century by Carlo I d'Angiò and later restored by Evangelista Menga who created corner ramparts and very steep walls, **Monopoli**'s castle, from Aragonese age with an annexed Roman tower and then besides **Villanova**'s fort, in the land of Ostuni, a well fortified town with imposing walls we also find the two castles of **Brindisi,** Forte a mare owing to Alfonso d'Aragona, dating back to the half of 15th century and Frederick's castle in the Seno di Ponente (Bay of

West).

We must go down towards Otranto, in the province of Lecce, in order to find another imposing castle, from Aragonese age and further south **Castro**'s castle, high, in the heart of the old town and falling sheer to the old walls. On the Ionian sea we find **Gallipoli**'s castle, from Angevin age, later rebuilt in the 16th century and fortified with the Rivellino (Ravelin), all surrounded with high walls, a further defence of the isle, where there was the town with typical lanes of Islamic town planning.

From Gallipoli we must reach **Taranto** in order to find another fortress on the sea

On this page: the Castle of Taranto and the revolving bridge.
On next page: the Castle of Bovino (*above*) and that of Otranto

from Aragonese age with subsequent reconstructions by two Renaissance great military architects: Francesco di Giorgio Martini and Ciro Ciri who used to work in Apulia. Beside the castle there is a revolving bridge, a great iron work achieved at the end of 19th century linking the old town (Where the Spartan colonists arrived and founded Taranto and where today we can admire the Doric columns, the only remains of Greeks) with the 19th century town exactly where the open sea meets with the Small sea.

It is worth visiting the old town so skilfully described by the great Riccardo Bacchelli in his "*L'Afrodite: un romanzo d'amore*" (*Aphrodite: a sentimental novel*): an old and very old, worn-out and shabby, strange knot of lanes and alleys and crossroads and narrow and meandering streets, with such open space as it lets the narrow streets and many dark passages and underground passages show up.

It was the result of thousand years of nobility and falls, grandeur and misfortunes, magnificence and dreariness, destructions and reconstructions…".

Inside the region we can

Conversano, the Castle of Marchione.
On previous page: the Castle of Lucera

find big and imposing castles everywhere. In the province of Foggia there are **Ascoli Satriano**'s castle, dating back to the 13th century, with subsequent transformations; **Bovino**'s built by the Norman Drogone, earl of Apulia, on the ruins of a Roman fortress, widened by Frederick II and later partly rebuilt by the Guevara dukes; **Deliceto**'s castle, of Norman origin, widened during Frederick age, later transformed and included into the town walls; **Lucera**'s castle, built on the ancient Roman acropolis by Frederick II, who had led twenty thousand Saracens into town, later included, between 1269 and 1283, by Carlo I d'Angiò into mighty town walls, about one kilometre long, with fifteen quadrangular towers and two circular ones among which Leonessa's tower distinguishing itself by an ashlar-worked base; **Monte Sant'Angelo**'s with the imposing Giants' Tower, originally Norman but with subsequent transformations and finally **Sant'Agata di Pu-glia**'s castle.

In the province of Bari, **Conversano**'s castle, even if it had been a widened and rebuilt defence work for many times it became, during Baroque time, a magnificent residence of the power-

ful Acquaviva d'Aragona family, feudatories from 1508 to 1806, who built a summer residence at **Marchione**, few kilometres far from the small town. Gioia del Colle's castle, with ashlar-worked covering, built by Normans on a previous Byzantine fortress, was subsequently restored by Frederick II and by the Angevines.

In the province of Brindisi we find Frederick's castle at Oria, with triangular plan where a rich collection of medieval arms is still preserved and from where Meyer-Graz wrote, "you can enjoy a wide and flourishing panorama… and from where you. Can notice the streets continuing to the infinite towards the East… In the far horizon the outline of Brindisi stands out and the blue strip of the Adriatic sea

The walls of Ostuni and, *below,* the Castle of Monte Sant'Angelo
On previous page: the Castle of Goia del Colle

shines".

At Carovigno there is Orsini del Balzo family's castle which later hosted Dentice di Frasso family; Mesagne's castle, ordered to be built by Roberto il Guiscardo and later redone; San Vito dei Normanni's castle, ordered to be built by Boemondo d'Altavilla. At Francavilla Fontana we can admire Imperiali family's palace, built in 1450 and widened one year later which has a rectangular plan with donjons on its corners: a splendid Baroque loggia "lightens" the mass of the building.

In the province of Lecce we must point out the impo-

Brindisi and Gallipoli
in *Kitab-i bahriye* by Piri Re'is

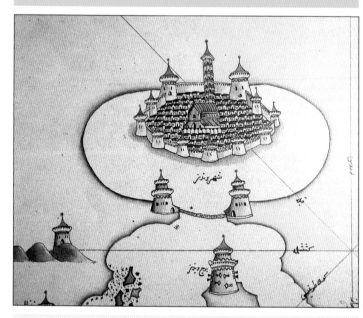

The port of Brindisi.
On next page: the town of Gallipoli

In the first decades of the 16th century Piri Re'is, a Turkish pirate, born in Gallipoli, Camali's grandson and Hayreddin Barbarossa's pupil became the admiral of the fleet of Sublime Door.

The sea was his life: as a pirate he raged along the coasts of the Mediterranean, assaulted cargo boats passing there, clashed with the scimitars dazzling in the sun, sequestrated, abducted and raped women in order to sell them at the slave market; as an admiral and in

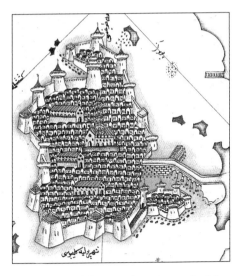

the ripe age, though he went on being adventurous and courageous he drew again the sea books (portolanos) he had together with some miniaturists giving way to a detailed cartographical work, the Kitab-I bahriye (sea book) which he gave to Solyman the Magnificent as a gift.

In the text referring to the images in the Kitab-I bahriye Piri Re'is describes the distances, the position of the towers, the rivers flowing into the sea, the shoals existing along the coastline, the ports and the coastal towns. From this description we can infer that the author knew the Mediterranean very well for crossing it everywhere. The Turkish pirate-admiral is supposed to have been in Apulia many times as he perfectly describes and draws all the coastline and some inland towns (We must remember the astonishing table of Gallipoli). As regards Brindisi he writes so: "...there is a very beautiful and big natural port which can host three or four hundred ships. Between this port and Valona (Avlona, in Albania) there are one hundred miles and from Valona as far as Otranto there are sixty miles. From Brindisi to Otranto there are forty miles. At the entrance of the port there is a rocky isle on which we find a small castle fortified with cannons. Foreign ships are not allowed to enter: the entrance of the port is closed with chains.

At the two ends of the chains there are two big towers with sentinels..." As regards Gallipoli "...(it is) on a small isle surrounded with the sea, but united to the continent through a bridge built on big stones. It often occurs that the waves increase so much that the above-mentioned bridge gets covered with the waters and the town seems to be located on an isle. It becomes higher and so it seems to be much stronger and storm proof.

Antonio Ventura, *L'Italia di Piri Re'is*, Capone Editore, 2000

The Castle of Acaia and, *below*, that of Massafra

sing trapezoidal castle of **Copertino**, with a wide moat and an imposing Angevin donjon, a 16th century work by Evangelista Menga, commissioned by Alfonso Castriota Scanderbeg, who strengthened the fortifications with a long defensive line dotted with twenty-three donjons. Acaia's castle, in these years mostly brought to light, is a work by Gian Giacomo dell'Acaia who fortified the Salentine small town with mighty walls and a wide moat. We find Nardò's castle, built by Giovanni Anto-

The Castle of Copertino and, *below*, that of Nardò

nio Acquaviva, rebuilt after the earthquake in 1700 and later changed in its front ;another in **Lecce** with the imposing Angevin donjon, the original construction around which, during Charles V's time there was the building of the fortification with trapezoidal plan and a wide moat thanks to dell'Acaia's plan.

In the province of Taranto we must remember **Massafra**'s castle, of Norman origin, which dominates one of the two ravines cutting across the town.

The towers

Between the 15th and 16th centuries, owing to the continuous assaults along the coasts, now on the part of the Saracen pirates, now of the opposite Dalmatia, Albania and Greek isles, now of the fleet of the Sublime Door, a series of watch towers were built along the whole coastline where other look-out posts had already been built in the past. Between 1558 and 1567, 339 look-out posts were built in the whole south and 96 in A-

Side: Leverano, Frederick's tower and, *below*, the tower and church of the farmhouse "li Nzarti" at Cavallino

On previous page:
Minervino tower, in the south of Otranto and Torre Lapillo in the Gulf of Taranto

pulia: 16 in the land of Bari, 80 in the land of Otranto.

We can still admire some cylindrical watch towers and quadrangular defensive towers, endowed with catapults, culverins and fire arms: some of which, brought to light, are in very good conditions while others are, unfortunately, in ruins. They are sometimes real fortresses, all sight communicating each other.

The coastal watchers, the tower-keepers plied between one tower and another and in case of enemy attack they were ready to alert the population by shining or sound signals (through bells, harquebus shots, horns) or directly.

Obviously no tower had an entrance at its base: it usually opened at a certain height and the entrance it-

Conversano, Castiglione tower

self was accessible from a ladder.

All the towers were endowed with a cistern where the rain water of the sun paving fell. Sometimes the cistern was inside the mighty walls of the sloping base of the tower. The girder defined a sort of ground floor where there was always a narrow entrance door. Some of these towers, especially the quadrangular ones, were endowed with very wide rooms and they could host many people, in case of sudden enemy attack. It was the age during which Ariadeno Barbarossa, Dragut, Occhialì and Curtogulo families, the pasha Lustambai, the renegade Cicala from Messina, at the head of pirates, often under the command of a power and another, plundered along the whole Apulian coast, assaulting villages and towns and capturing prisoners later sold as slaves at the market of East.

We do not find the towers only along the coast: there are also many in the inhabited places, now included in the following towns: Bitonto with the Angevine tower, Castellana Grotte where the Norman tower becomes the bell-tower of the mother church, Cisternino with the Bishop's tower or Town tower. Like the coastal towers they were watch and also defensive towers..

The prehistory
The dinosaurs as the first inhabitants

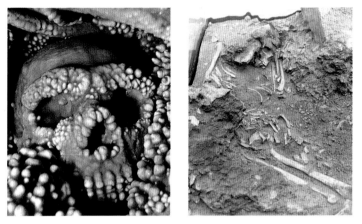

The man from Altamura and, *right*, the woman from Ostuni

Since the mists of time Apulia has been inhabited and crowded with man. Two findings bear witness to it: in 1993 "the man from Altamura", a human fossil dating back to the end of Pleistocene period (200.000 years before) and even earlier, in 1991 Delia, "the pregnant woman from Ostuni", preserved in the local Museum of pre-classical civilisations, dating back to 25.000 years ago. The two exceptional recent prehistoric findings, the human and animal fossils, the graffiti, the tools of the man from Palaeolithic age brought to light in the Romanelli Cave, near Castro in the Salento, the pictograms in the Deer Cave at Porto Badisco and those in the Gargano caves, first Paglicci, the tools and prehistoric objects at Altamura, but also at Molfetta, the so-called "Veneri" (Venuses) of Parabita, the menhirs (many in the area of Lecce), the dolmens and the specchie (moulds), are all very precious marks coming from ancient times. In the area of Giurdignano, in the province of Lecce, there is the greatest quantity of megaliths of Italy: 14 menhirs and 7 dolmens; the menhir in the most northern part is Canosa's, about three metres

Porto Badisco, pictograms in Deer's Cave and, *below*, Siponto.
On next page, from high: Menhir of Giurdignano, "One thousand stones" of Patu' and menhir of Cavallino

high, while the most imposing dolmens are at Bisce-
glie, in the area of Lecce (at
Giurdignano as well as Me-
lendugno where there are
two) and in the area of Brindisi, the so-called "Paladins'
Table" on Ostuni-Fasano
road: it is three metres long,
one and half metres wide
while the slab is the slab is
three metres wide and two
metres long.

A "more well-develo-

Dolmen Li Scusi on Minervino- Uggiano La Chiesa road.
On next page: Dolmen La Chianca on Risceglie-Corato road
and the trace of dinosaur on the Gargano

ped" dolmen, as some scholars say, could be "one hundred stone" of **Patù**, an original construction made up of enormous blocks of stones which form a small singular temple opposite the Byzantine church of San Giovanni.

Other marks of the past are the specchie (moulds) present in the whole region (we must remember the big six-step mould of *Pozzo Stramuzzo* at **Castellana Grotte**, *Moors' mould* on the road which from Caprarica leads to Martano, in the province of Lecce and at **Ceglie Messapica**, in the province of Brindisi, which, included into the massive walls, must have represented the defensive system of the ancient built-up area).

But in Apulia we can find marks prior to the prehistoric age thanks to the latest revolutionary findings of "traces" of dinosaurs at Altamura, on the Murgia, endowed with dry stones and at San Marco in Lamis, on the Gargano.

Those traces bear witness to the emersion of our region out of waters and they prove, as the archaeologist Donata Venturo confirms, that between 120 and 65 millions of years, Apulia was inhabited by dinosaurs everywhere. This situation completely changes the traditional geographical concept of the area because it means that Apulia was out of waters and today's inland **Altamura**, represented the coast of a marshy terrain,

full of vegetation as they had to "feed" many dinosaurs (the palaeontologists say that each dinosaur needed 30-40 hectares of grassland per week). We can notice the traces of forty dinosaurs in Pontrelli Cave at Altamura extending for 12.000 square metres. They were supposed to move quietly in an only direction along a stream or along the coast which must have linked the region with Istria and Dalmatia.

From high, clockwise: the Giant of Barletta, the lighthouse of Leuca, the bell-tower of Soleto and that of Monte Sant'Angelo

From high, clockwise: the clock tower of
Martina Franca, the Obelisk of Lecce, the
column of Sant'Oronzo at Ostuni, votive
chapel of San Dana in the province of Lecce

An open museum

Lucera, the amphitheatre and, *below*, Canosa, the mosaic of the Basilica of San Leucio. *On next page:* jewels preserved in the museum of Taranto

The whole Apulia, from north to south, is an endless archaeological area bearing witness to a well-planned human life, before the Greeks' arrival and the Roman conquest. We must consider the towns belonging to Apulian, Peucetian and Messapian people; the Apulian, Magno-Greek pottery of *Gnathia*: elegant and refined objects preserved in the Archaeological museum of Taranto: this all gives the idea of what Apulia was.

We must add **Lucera**'s archaeological area with the amphitheatre from Augustan age, built on a sloping terrain, 127 metres long and 95 metres wide, which could host from 16 thousand to 18 thousand spectators; **Canosa**'s archaeo-

logical area and the remains of the 5th–6th century Basilica of San Leucio, with enormous capitals and parts of mosaics, the arch in honour of Terenzio Varrone; **Manfredonia**'s area with its museum where the mysterious Daunian stele are preserved (7th-6th centuries BC); **Siponto**'s; **Arpi**'s with the line of walls and the caved tombs, a town destroyed

On this page: Canne della Battaglia.
On next page: Egnazia and, *below,* Herdonia

by Saracens in the 11th century and an important place of the ancient Apulia, allied to Romans against Samnites and conquered by Hannibal after the battle of Canne. There is also **Herdonia**'s archaeological area, lapped by the Carapelle, on Traiana Way, a high commercial centre of the past, a Daunian built-up area which later became a Roman *municipium*: we can admire the remains of the Forum, the pa-

ved square surrounded with columns and the rests of a circular market; **Canne**'s archaeological area where Hannibal defeated Romans in 216 BC: on the hill we can see what remains of the temples, streets, columns and ancient homes as well as the imposing town walls rebuilt in early Middle Age and later razed to the ground in 1083 by Roberto il Guiscardo. We also must remember **Ruvo**'s area

with the splendid Jatta museum which preserves the attic vase representing the death of Thalos, a mythical guardian of Crete ("If the museum did not exist- Ferdinand Gregorovius unfairly says while travelling throughout Apulia at the end of 19th century – Ruvo would not be so important and the foreigner would never set foot there"); **Gravina**'s archaeological area with Botromagno's hill; **Gioia del Colle**, with Sannace Mount, the ancient *Turum* of Plinium and going southwards the big archaeological area of **Egnazia**, once *Gnathia*, with the rests of the important port from which the Roman legions sailed for the East, the rests of the walls, of the Forum and the interesting built-up area. **Taranto** was the capital of Magna Graecia: of its ancient splendour only few things remain unfortunately (roomed tombs, some floor mosaic, rests of the aqueduct and of walls) owing to the continuous transforma-

Taranto, the Doric columns in the old town and, *below*, the Daunia stele.
On next page: Mesagne, the crater and Manduria, the necropolis

tions throughout the centuries which have completely covered all things from Magno-Greek and Roman ages. In the south east of Taranto there is

Mesagne, an important Messapian town, on the Appian Way, half way between Taranto and Brindisi, with the imposing roomed tombs (great is the "tomb of the Prince", kept in the new rooms of the museum with the splendid pottery included in it), some of which have been just recently brought to light in the heart of the town.

From the port of both the ancient *Brundusium* and Egnazia people sailed for the East: of the port and the town only few things unfortunately remain (a theatre was built on a wide part of the ancient town brought to light many years before!) even if we can visit the museum very rich in findings brought to light in the whole area.

We are already in the an-

cient Messapia. Here it is worth visiting **Manduria** with its great necropolis and threefold walls which surrounded and still partly surround the town, under which the Spartan king Archidamo died; Roca, in the Salento with the wide archaeological area and Poetry Cave (once a pagan temple devoted to the god *Tautor*) with hundreds of engravings on the walls in Messapian, Greek and Latin which still appear; **Lecce**, once *Lupiae* with the amphitheatre mostly still covered with later buildings and *Rudiae*, few kilometres far from the town, Ennio's mother-country, with

Alezio, the walls and, *below*, the amphitheatre of Lecce.
On next page: Roca and the Zeus of Ugento

its neglected archaeological area. In the south of the province of Lecce we find **Ugento**, with parts of the Messapian walls, a small town where a bronze statue of Zeus, dating back to the 5th century BC was brought to light some years before, and it is now preserved in the museum of Taranto; **Vaste**, **Alezio**, **Muro Leccese** are all Messapian towns where we can still admire, like at Cavallino, within a stone's throw from the capital, parts of the ancient walls which are sometimes in very good conditions.

At **Vaste** we must visit the small but interesting museum which, among other things, preserves one of the most beautiful collections of ancient coins kept in a container brought to light during the latest excavations.

A Region of believers
with great Sanctuaries and rupestrian churches

Apulia is also a region of believers. St. Peter landed at Leuca and other resorts before reaching Rome, here the first Palaeochristian churches were built.

The Gargano, the "holy mountain", has always been

On previous page: Monte Sant'Angelo, the Palatine Basilica.
On this page: San Giovanni Rotondo and Monte Sant'Angelo

an attraction for the believers from all over the world: since the Middle Ages, along the *Holy Road of Longobards* the pilgrims from any part of Europe have gone to pray into the grotto of St. Michael's sanctuary (at **Monte Sant'Angelo**) where the Archangel had appeared between 490 and 493 AC; there, even San Francesco d'Assisi went up as pilgrim in 1216. (Near there we must visit the 13th century church of Santa Maria Maggiore and the so-called Tomb of Rotari). Nowadays, still along the Holy Road of Longobards, other millions of believers go to San Giovanni Rotondo, into the sanctuary

The *college*
of San Nicola di Casole

Otranto, the small Byzantine church of St. Peter

In the south of Otranto, taking the coastal road leading to Porto Badisco, the mythical bay where Enea is supposed to have landed, and to Santa Cesarea, a famous seaside resort and spa, before the radar position of the Military Aeronautics, turning right in a private property, crossing a long road planted with trees, we can face a farmhouse built on the few ruins of the church of San Nicola di Casole.

Nothing remains (except for some parts of the columns of the ancient church) of the monastery and other rooms which once hosted the monks who, as soon as the bell rang, at dawn, used to pray, to take care of the fields, to copy classical Greek and Latin texts.

The monastery of San Nicola di Casole was established in 1098 by Boemondo I and his mother Costanza. It was Boemondo that gave the farmhouse of Casole as a gift to a group of hermits led by Joseph, the first "igumeno" of the future monastery and Boemondo himself subsidized the building of the above-mentioned monastery, which became a meaningful fact from both the political and religious points of view.

In a few years' time Casole

became a sort of English college –Cesare Daquino wrote in his "Bizantini in Terra d'Otranto" (Capone 2000)- where they offered teaching, board and lodging free to people who were interested in Greek literature and philosophy as well as in Latin Classics.

Otranto, in that time, was a sort of outpost of the Greek church in the peninsula and the local archbishop's seat was under Constantinople: this explains the deep relationship with te East.

At Casole the monks, dressing a wide black tunic with hood of the same colour, devoted themselves to prayer and study: they had got a big library, the supreme good of the coenobium and they reproduced the great works of the past led by the protocalligrapher who superintended the copyists.

The coenobium of Casole, which had got its "branches" all over the Terra d'Otranto (the so

called metochie), became a link with the Eastern world with which it has kept a close relationship for about four centuries.

This was due to the skills and authoritativeness of the "igumeni" (the abbots) to whom all the monks owed obedience and respect.

Casole, in August of 1480, after that the Turks assaulted Otranto fiercely, was put to fire and sword: the monks of the monastery were killed, their furnishings were burnt and many documents which had been jealously preserved were destroyed.

Today, in spite of the accurate studies, we know very little of the great book-inheritance even if many volumes, which had miraculously escaped the destroying fury of the Ottoman soldiers, are preserved in famous Italian and foreign libraries.

Foggia, the Sanctuary of the Crowned Virgin and, *below*, the inside of the Sanctuary of Leuca. *On next page:* Leuca, the Sanctuary and Massafra, Madonna della Scala

of Santa Maria delle Grazie, built by Capuchins in order to visit San Pio da Pietralcina's tomb where they invoke the Saint of the Stigmata. The sanctuary, after the Madonna of Guadalupe's in Mexico, is one of the most visited Catholic sanctuaries in the world.

The new church is being built thanks to Renzo Piano's plan and the believers' charity and it will host ten thousand believers.

In Daunia another sanctuary, destination for many pilgrims is Madonna dell'Incoronata's, few kilometres far from Foggia.

It was built where in 1001 first the prince of Ariano and then an old shepherd, while being in the wood along the Cervaro, saw the Madonna on an oak-tree in all Her splendour.

In the deep south of the region, at **Santa Maria di Leuca** we find the sanctuary of the Madonna of *Finibus Terrae*, built on an ancient pagan temple devoted to Minerva where thousands of pilgrims arrive from any part of the world. Famous people visited the sanctuary such as: San Francesco d'Assisi and St. Peter of whom remains a cross(the so-called *St. Peter's cross*) in the opposite square. We also must remember Giovanni Paolo II's

Castellaneta and, *below*, Massafra, a ravine.
On previous page: Mottola, the village of Petruscio, Vaste and Ortelle

visit in 1990. The church, often destroyed by Saracens and Turks has always been rebuilt.

In the past and even nowadays there are the small welcoming hypogeal churches, marks of faith and civilisation. They are sculpted in the tufaceous rock or along the slopes of the ravines, especially in the area of Taranto, but also in the Salento. Around the year thousand the so-called "rupestrian civilization" developed in Apulia owing to coenobitical people who had fled from the East for the iconoclastic persecution caused by Leone III Isaurico (717-741), a Byzantine empe-

ror. At **Massafra**, **Mottola**, **Castellaneta**, **Laterza** these monks together with the ecclesiastical communities, digging into the slopes of the steep natural chasms, built houses, streets, places of cult where unknown artists, using the technique of fresco painted the Pantocrator while blessing in the Greek way, the Madonna, the saints, scenes from the Old and New Testament. They gave origin to the southern Byzantine art as the fact concerned all the south even if in the areas of Taranto and Salento it achieved very good results.

At **Mottola**, in the ravine of Petruscio, we can admire, in a unique and wild environment, the town sculpted in the rock along the walls of the canal and we must al-

On this page and on previous one: Mottola, San Nicola dei Greci

Massafra, the crypt of Buona Nuova: San Vito and Santa Caterina (14th century).
On next page: Giurdignano, the crypt of San Salvatore and, *below,* Poggiardo, the Museum of crypts

so visit the crypts in the area of Casalrotto to realise the magnificence of Apulian Byzantine art. At Casalrotto it is worth reaching the *crypt of San Nicola dei Greci*, recently visited by orthodox Greek and Russian pilgrims. Here, in the very silent ravines, we can see the excavation made into the tufaceous rock in order to build the place of cult adorned with frescoed walls and pillars, still in good conditions. At **Massafra**, after visiting the sanctuary of the Madonna della Scala, going down the ravine, we notice small churches, houses, underground passages, frescoes and architectural buildings such as the so-called chemistry of Greguro the wizard. In the Salento we

must go to **Carpignano Salentino**, into the crypt of Saints Marina and Cristina, in the central square of the village, in order to admire the most ancient Byzantine frescoes with date and signature: a great Christ Pantocrator, signed by Teofilato and a series of saints, one of which is signed by Eustazio, with big eyes, flowing drapery and very vivid colours ranging from the blue to the purple red, the yellow, the ochre and the white. At **Giurdignano** San Salvatore's crypt has been recently

Galatina, Santa Caterina d'Alessandria, frescoes

brought to light. It is very architecturally interesting, it has one nave and two aisles and few traces of frescoes which can hardly be seen.

At **Otranto**, along the steep slope of the Valley of Memory, but also in the town, we can see the rests of the typical hypogeal crypts where unfortunately what remains is very little. At **Poggiardo** the museum of Villa Episcopo preserves the 13th century frescoes, taken off from Santa Maria degli Angeli's crypt and restored, a building sculpted in the tufaceous rock near the mother church. At **San Vito dei Normanni**, in the areas of **Fasano**, at **Monopoli**, as well as at **Gravina** and **Altamura**, (at Jesce exactly) we can visit tens and tens of well kept frescoes because they have been skilfully restored and located in places easy to reach.

The baroque

Lecce, Santa Croce, detail of the front

Apulia is also the region of Baroque art thanks to **Lecce** and **Martina Franca** in particular.

In **Lecce** we can find the Basilica of Santa Croce with its superabundant front but also the front of the Seminary, at Duomo square as well as the noble palaces which, between 17th and 18th centuries the powerful local families had them built in the town. The fact which is unknown to the other Apulian towns, takes an important aspect in the capital of the Salento for the easiness

Lecce, Santa Croce, detail of the front

to work the local stone (lec-cisu). Anyone, walking down the small streets of the old part of the town and looking upwards, stands o-pen-mouthed and cannot help admiring the crenella-ted balconies, the small putti following one another on the twisted columns of the al-tars, thousands of strange fi-gures supporting corbels, ar-chitraves, trabeations: for the flourishing of the architectu-re the town has been defined the "Florence of the South". People coming from north and going southwards are charmed by the monumental wealth coming out of the Ba-roque art: it has Spanish ori-gins owing to Iberian people who left significant marks in the architecture as well as in the language and customs. We also must consider some exceptions such as von Ried-sel who, in a letter to Win-ckelmann, defines "execra-ble" this kind of architecture and "unbearable the small and endlessly superabun-dant ornaments".

Lecce, Seminary Palace
Below: Martina Franca, St. Michael's Church

Martina Franca
A different town by Gianni Custodero

Martina Franca is not like the others: here even local people always want to distinguish themselves by everything…

After passing through the gate, near the ducal palace, in the small triangular square, it is not easy to find a common link between Baroque and manufacturing industry, the culture of wine and the taste of new.

We must visit the palace. The front is supposed to be sculptured by Bernini: the duke Petraccone V Caracciolo is said to have paid six thousand ducats in order to build it, a dizzy amount of money even for a lord of the 17th century. Inside the 18th century frescoes by Domenico Carella and his brothers harmonise lime-like colours with the taste and culture of the age: is this the secret of Martina Franca people?

From the palace to San Martino, the "ring", the narrow main street which has always represented the heart of the town life gives the same impression: the past meets the present without shocking the eye, in harmony with the ancient balance of these people. This also regards the Baroque which recalls better the skills of the stone-cutters than the violent expressions of forms, figures and vaults similar to those in Naples and Spain.

The style is also different from that existing in Lecce and not only because the stone is different.

There is an innate sobriety which balances everything and in the narrow alleys melting of lime and cleanness the presence of the luxury house does not seem unfaòiliar but it is included in the context and milieu.

The Baroque of Martina Franca seems more suitable to decorations than to monuments…

…San Martino, with the front, the small square with the portico, the university palace with clock, the

other "palaced" houses, as we can read in ancient documents: all corners to be discovered or re-discovered. Has Martina got a Baroque soul? Or under a good dress suiting a sober fashion, there is a rustic soul, is not there? But it is better to deal with the dress and refer to manufacturing and people working in this field which has an important role in the economy of Martina.

As regards wine, instead, the white one is well preserved: the worked grapes are verdeca and the white from Alessano, like for the Locorotondo. In Martina they produce other wines of very good quality and they even bottle the Aglianico.

Some years ago a serious industrialist made people notice that the grapes born here, after being exported to France, used to be imported with the label and the prestige of the champagne.

Impressions, news and records follow one another.

As regards the horse-riding there are four riding-grounds and the horse from Murge. There is also the ass from Martina Franca, bred in this area and wich once accompanied the peasants in their tiring days…

The landscape

The landscape shows a different situation because if we go through it from north to south and from east to west we will notice a more different variety of land than the other regions'. We can pass from the Tavoliere, a great flat extent of ground as far as the eye can see, where once millions of sheep going down from Abruzzo and Basilicata winter used to the middle hill which in some its parts faces the sea and we can finally see again the plain in the Salento. From east to west, as Apulia is a narrow land, we can pass, through few kilometres from the coast to the hills of Murgia, an immense inhabited little bare area which is dry in summer while it shows only few tufts of grass in spring.

This is the Apulian Karst area where as soon as the waters fall they are swallowed up by the subsoil. This is the region where we find the great underground grottoes which have developed for many centuries in the bowels of the earth: a natural phenomenon like Postumia's which can be seen at Castellane Grotte. Here there are kilometres of underground passages where, among stalactites and stalagmites, in an unreal silence, we can see the greatness of

The Apulian countryside and *below*, the Pulicchio, few kilometres far from Altamura
On next page: Bovino, the sanctuary of Valleverde, the Laghi Alimini

nature. We cannot help referring to another landscape even if it is less relevant but equally suggestive that is the **Zinzulusa**, a grotto near Castro, in the province of Lecce.

Along some dolinas we can find Aleppo pine-trees, oak-groves, carob-trees and woody areas which unfortunately during the centuries have become narrower owing to the indiscriminate deforestations.

At **Tricase** we keep astonished in front of the great specimen of valonia oak, today existing in Italy.

What remains of the great woods where the brigands used to shelter? We can still find parts of the **Pianelle**

Wood, between Martina Franca and Massafra; there is also the **Mercadante Forest**, created by man, between Cassano Murge and Altamura. We must go to the Gargano and along the **Daunian Subapennines** in order to enjoy an unpolluted nature. In the **Umbra Forest,** which has become a National Park, we can find big woods rich in maples, ilexes, beeches, all of them ivy-mantled, real arboreal monuments standing out against the sky, with rare kinds of birds flying among them. Instead, the undergrowth, rich in some botanical species hosts roe-bucks, beech-martens, badgers, foxes, wild boars.

Subapennines are as rich as Umbra Forest as it has high and wide green plains and many-coloured hilly slopes.

The secular woods, with an undergrowth rich in vegetation, are the reign of wild boars, but it is not unusual to see the eagles flying about in the sky. In this wonderful landscape, run through by streams and valleys (we must remember the Bovino Bridge, reign of the brigands till the end of the 19th century) we find small interesting communities, with their uses and customs as well as, as it happens in **Faeto** and **Celle San Vito**, those speaking their own language that is the Provencal.

A great quantity of lakes existing in the region and all communicating with the Adriatic sea belongs to the coastal landscape.

In the north, at the foot of the Gargano, we find Lakes **Lesina** and **Varano**, twenty

Here and on previous page
Images from Monte Sant'Angelo

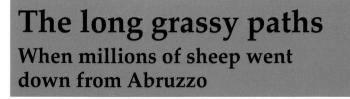

The long grassy paths
When millions of sheep went down from Abruzzo

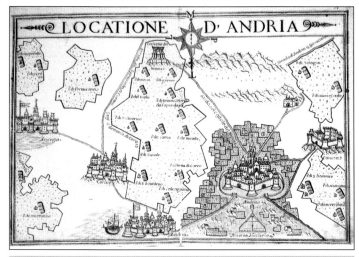

"Locatione di Andria" (*above*) and "Locatione di Castiglione"
from *Atlante delle Locazioni* (1686) by Antonio and Nunzio Michele

Today who walks through the plain of Foggia will notice hundreds of hectares of land without any woods or trees. The olive and vine yards as well as the orchards have been planted recently.

We cannot see here the olive which, instead, in Apulia dominates with its age log trees: the olive-yards are young and recently planted.

In this plain, destined for pasture, it was not allowed people to plant trees and shrubs because they thought that the ground would get dry and the grass could be damaged.

It is in this wide area that the grass was the main food for millions of sheep which passed through the "tratturi" (natural paths for sheep), 111 metres wide, in winters coming from the mountains of Abruzzo, Molise, Basilicata, Campania as well as from those of Apulian Murge. The transhumance has been for ages source of life for thousands of peasants and shepherds of the South and high source of income for the Reign.

Practised since the ancient time the transhumance was regulated by Alfonso I d'Aragona through the institution of Regia Dogana della Mena delle Pecore (Royal Custom of Passage of

Sheep), first in Lucera as seat, then in Foggia. It lasted from 1447 to 1806 even if the situation went on till the second half of the 19th period when, for the low economic importance of stock-raising and the dissolution of the ties of pasture weighing on the Tavoliere, the transhumance lost its economic power. Today it no more happens.

Very little remains of the "tratturi", the long grassy paths extending from the mountain to the plain: first for the usurpations, then for the decision to cultivate that land there is no sign of the "tratturi".

The longest (244 kilometres) was the tratturo of the King, linking L'Aquila to Foggia. That leading from Foggia to Celano, reaching Lucera for 15 kilometres was 207 kilometres long; that which went from Candela to Pescasseroli was 211 kilometres long. That leading from Lucera to Castel di Sangro was 127 kilome-

tres long, that linking Melfi to Castellaneta was 142 kilometres long.

These very long "motorways" with many wide stops (resting places) met each other forming a real roadway where bailiffs, young and old shepherds with big white dogs moved and during the passage they used to place at the head and on the sides of the herd. Some days earlier they reached the stops where they prepared for the milking, the production of the milk or, when possible, for the shearing.

Then a real market took place before the presence of spectacled customs officers who controlled the situation so that the "owners of the firm" could pay the fida (land let for grazing) for the lease.

Italo Palasciano, *Le lunghe vie erbose. Tratturi e pastori del Sud*, Capone 1999
Antonio e Nunzio Michele, *Atlante delle Locazioni*, Capone 1989

The sea of Leuca and, *below,* Torre dell'Alto
On next page: Ciolo bridge and, *below,* Santa Cesarea Terme

kilometres long and three kilometres wide the former while the latter is ten kilometres long and eight kilometres wide. In the south, near Otranto, we find Lakes Alimini, smaller than Lesina and Varano. We can also find natural oasis along the coastline everywhere such as: **Frattarolo** preserve in the south of Manfredonia; the natural sea preserve at **Torre Guaceto**, in the area of Brindisi; at **Rauccio**, in the area of Lecce, at **Cesine**, near Vernole. We can also remember on the Ionian side the natural park of **Porto Selvaggio-Torre Uluzzo**: all of them are wide marshy areas

except for Porto Selvaggio which, among lacustrine plants and thickets hosts many rare migratory birds as well as permanent game.

Along the coastline there are the **salt-works of Margherita di Savoia** among Zapponeta, Trinitapoli and the homonymous resort: 4.0000 hectares, with 500 basins, twenty kilometres of length, tons of produced sea salt and an unusual and suggestive landscape.

Castellana Grotte

"This is the Karst of the South; grottoes and caverns bore it (...) for twenty years of these grottoes (*nella foto:* Castro, La Zinzulusa) we have known only a round chasm similar to an enormous well, surrounded with ilexes and opening on the hill.

Popular superstitions considered it the reign of the hell. Franco Anelli from the Institute of Spelaeology which once had the seat in Postumia, after letting himself down into the chasm in 1938 found out in the wall the corridor through which he opened the underground passage and so the scientific exploration started. The grottoes were settled the following year, but the real official opening took place in 1949.(...) Castellana's underground reign has less wide rooms than Postumia's, but longer and more mysterious corridors.

There are more magnificence of alabasters, more varieties of strangeness, thick pieces of stalactites. We find many transparent walls where the stone becomes so much thin as to imitate the mould and the veil. There are also ceilings of stalactites of incomparable whiteness.

Guido Piovene, *Viaggio in Italia*, Baldini & Castoldi, 1993

The Tremiti islands

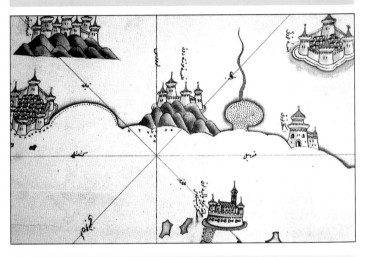

The Tremiti Islands on the maps of the trurkish admiral Piri Re' Is

Destination for tourists owing to their wealth of sea and land, the Tremiti Islands, which form, together with other two reefs, the small archipelago were known on ancient maps as Insulae Diomedae as a memento of the Greek hero who is supposed to have been buried on these isles.

Inhabited for ages, they have been intended to be a sort of prison for political internees: among other things they "hosted" many Libyan people that is why some years before Gheddafi claimed their "ownership".

Of the three isles San Nicola's, the smallest, is also the most populated. It is the seat of Town Hall and it hosts an interesting Benedictine abbey, Santa Maria's, dating back to the 11th century: a rich and powerful abbey which, in its splendour, was endowed with a fleet, it hosted peregrines going by sea towards the Gargano to the sanctuary of Michael the Archangel and it regulated the civil life of the islanders. A building which, during the centuries, has suffered many changes but that has kept the original structure with its walls and bastions.

San Domino was once rich in flourishing vegetation and pine-woods of which some parts remain in spite of the building "assault". Today it is very fertile and greatly used by local farmers. Instead, the Capraia Isle is desert and abandoned.

The coasts falling sheer to the sea reveal surprise in the ravines and grottes facing the blue sea rich in fauna which today is fortunately.

Being protected as it reppresents a natural preserve.

Under the "Trulli" of Alberobello

The "trulli" have always been one of the most singular tourist attractions of Apulia. Alberobello representing the capital of the "trulli" owing to its two monumental quarters can be reached through the Valley of Itria: many kilometres among hills, dry-stone walls, vines, almond-trees, cherry-orchards, thickets, strips of land taken from the rock through an action lasting for many million years. It is here, among these hills that the houses with cone-shaped domes, as Piovene defined then, appear more frequently as soon as we go towards Alberobello. They a-re the so called "trulli", with their pinnacles and grey stone where old and magic white-lime marks follow one a-nother as for game. At Albe-robello, starting from Largo Martellotta we find a fairy-like scenery: we keep really spellbound. It is impossible to find a similar place in the world and that is why Unesco, in 1996, included the capital of trulli among the goods representing the inheritance of mankind.

The architecture of the trullo is extremely simple and its structure is plain.

It was due to the local peasants who built with the

Alberobello, Trullo Sovrano

local "chiancarelle" (calcareous stone ashlars which are about seven centimetres thick), these comfortable and spartan buildings, cool in summer, warm in winter; the habit of building has always taken the thermic variations into consideration. The base of the trullo, be it quadrangular or be it circular, once in dry stone, is today a masonry and from a certain height onwards, from 1.50 to 2 metres, without any mortar, the "chiancherelle" jut out

inside for about 2 metres, reaching the apex of the cone closed by a small round slab or a high decorative pinnacle which can take the form of a disk, a star, a sphere sometimes supported by a cross. We do not know their origin, however, contribute to the Apulian Eastern art.

In the valley of Itria we find other characteristic villages which are worth visiting as they are in the surroundings.

Locorotondo, famous for

Martina Franca and, *below*, Ostuni, the arch of the Bishop's Palace
On next page: Cisternino and, *below*, Locorotondo

the production of the local white wine whose name derives from the place, is located on a low relief: we can notice it from afar owing to its circular town-planning structure and to the dome of its church dominating it; **Cisternino**, with its white houses, is a kind of balcony facing the valley; **Ostuni**, the white town, facing not the valley of Itria but the Adriatic sea, located on a hill, surrounded with long parts of medieval walls, stands out for its white houses. Some kilometres further there are its two seaside resorts, from Pilone and Rosamarina as

far as Villanova and further. **Martina Franca**, famous for its old part and the Baroque churches (the collegiate church of San Martino and the church of San Domenico) and noble palaces, but also for the ducal palace hosting the paintings of Domenico Carella in magnificent rooms.

Martina Franca is also famous for the festival of the valley of Itria, a great kermess of lyrical and symphonic music which represents an attraction for music lovers from all over the world.

Ceglie Messapica, whose name shows its pre-Roman origin, has got a museum hosting significant findings which have been brought to light during the years.

The east once again

Other towns recalling the East once again are Leuca, Cenate at Nardò, villa Sticchi at Santa Cesarea Terme. The Byzantine East is well represented in St. Peter's church in the heart of the old part of Otranto even if it refers to the East ten centuries before while the later one can be admired in the villas in various styles in Apu-

Santa Maria di Leuca, villa De Francesco and, *below*, villa Serafini Sauli
On previous page: Santa Cesarea Terme, villa Sticchi
and, *below*, Santa Maria di Leuca, villa Episcopo

lia, but especially in the Salento.

Thanks to a wealthy middle class as well as local aristocratic families, at the end of the 19th century and in the first decades of the 20th century, buildings in Pompeian, neo-Classical and eastern styles were built in well located coastal areas of the Salento as well as in Lecce and its surroundings.

The most expressive building regarding the architecture and colours is certainly

San Cesario, villa Terragno
On previous page: Santa Maria al Bagno, le Cenate, villa Gaballo
and, *below*, villa del Vescovo

villa Sticchi at Santa Cesarea Terme, with a dome as great as those existing in Istambul, with its crenellated balconies and the mixture of decorations. It has got a loggia severely surrounded with spiral-shaped thin columns and many other details like something out of the Arabian Nights. In **Santa Maria di Leuca** we also find very interesting villas such as: villa Mellacqua, villa De Francesco, villa Episcopo, villa Serafini Sauli, villa Daniele and, in Lecce, villa Martini, villa Himera, villa Indraccolo; at San Cesario, villa Terragno and villa Fazzi as well as those at Cenate, Nardò.

A suggestive Eastern model in the heart of Apulia is the minaret, in **Fasano** Forest, achieved in the first half of the 20th century by the painter and caricaturist Damasco Bianchi from Bari as a holiday castle.

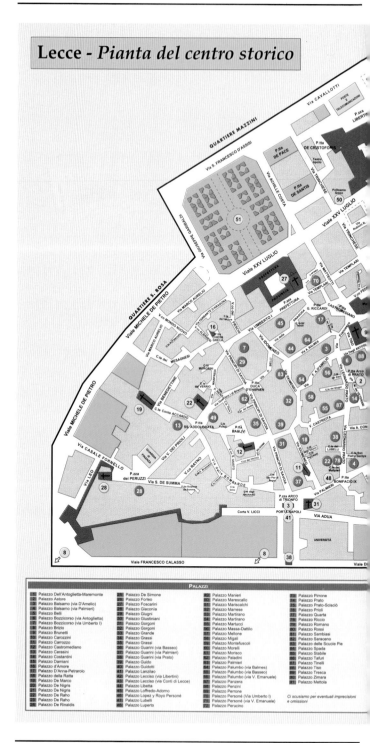

Lecce - *Pianta del centro storico*

PALAZZI

1. Palazzo Dell'Antoglietta-Maremonte
2. Palazzo Astore
3. Palazzo Balsamo (via D'Amelio)
4. Palazzo Balsamo (via Palmieri)
5. Palazzo Belli
6. Palazzo Bozzicorso (via Antoglietta)
7. Palazzo Bozzicorso (via Umberto I)
8. Palazzo Brizio
9. Palazzo Brunetti
10. Palazzo Carozzini
11. Palazzo Carozzo
12. Palazzo Castromediano
13. Palazzo Cesarini
14. Palazzo Costantini
15. Palazzo Damiani
16. Palazzo d'Amore
17. Palazzo D'Anna-Petrarolo
18. Palazzo della Ratta
19. Palazzo De Marco
20. Palazzo De Nigris
21. Palazzo De Nigris
22. Palazzo De Raho
23. Palazzo De Raho
24. Palazzo De Rinaldis
25. Palazzo De Simone
26. Palazzo Forleo
27. Palazzo Foscarini
28. Palazzo Giaconia
29. Palazzo Giugni
30. Palazzo Giustiniani
31. Palazzo Gorgoni
32. Palazzo Gorgoni
33. Palazzo Grande
34. Palazzo Grassi
35. Palazzo Grassi
36. Palazzo Guarini (via Basseo)
37. Palazzo Guarini (via Palmieri)
38. Palazzo Guarini (via Prato)
39. Palazzo Guido
40. Palazzo Guidotti
41. Palazzo Lanzilao
42. Palazzo Lecciso (via Libertini)
43. Palazzo Lecciso (via Conti di Lecce)
44. Palazzo Libetta
45. Palazzo Loffredo-Adorno
46. Palazzo Lopez y Royo Personé
47. Palazzo Lubelli
48. Palazzo Luperto
49. Palazzo Manieri
50. Palazzo Marescallo
51. Palazzo Mariscalchi
52. Palazzo Marrese
53. Palazzo Martirano
54. Palazzo Martirano
55. Palazzo Martucci
56. Palazzo Massa-Dattilo
57. Palazzo Mellone
58. Palazzo Migali
59. Palazzo Montefuscoli
60. Palazzo Morelli
61. Palazzo Morisco
62. Palazzo Paladini
63. Palazzo Palmieri
64. Palazzo Palumbo (via Balmes)
65. Palazzo Palumbo (via Basseo)
66. Palazzo Palumbo (via V. Emanuele)
67. Palazzo Panzera
68. Palazzo Penzini
69. Palazzo Perrone
70. Palazzo Persone (Via Umberto I)
71. Palazzo Persone (via V. Emanuele)
72. Palazzo Perucino
73. Palazzo Pirrone
74. Palazzo Prato
75. Palazzo Prato-Scisciò
76. Palazzo Prioli
77. Palazzo Quarta
78. Palazzo Riccio
79. Palazzo Romano
80. Palazzo Rossi
81. Palazzo Sambiasi
82. Palazzo Saraceno
83. Palazzo delle Scuole Pie
84. Palazzo Spada
85. Palazzo Stabile
86. Palazzo Tafuri
87. Palazzo Tinelli
88. Palazzo Tiso
89. Palazzo Tresca
90. Palazzo Zimara
91. Palazzo Mettola

Ci scusiamo per eventuali imprecisioni e omissioni

MONUMENTI E CHIESE

1 Anfiteatro romano
2 Arco di Prato
3 Arco di Trionfo
4 Biblioteca
5 Campanile
6 Castello di Carlo V
7 Cattedrale
8 Chiesa dei SS. Niccolò e Cataldo
9 Chiesa del Gesù (Buon Consiglio)
10 Chiesa della Madonna
di Dio e S. Nicola
11 Chiesa della Nove
12 Chiesa delle Alcantarine
(S. Maria della Provvidenza)
13 Convento delle Paolotte ora
Palazzo di Città
14 Chiesa di S. Eligio
15 Chiesa di S. Francesco
della Scarpa
16 Chiesa di S. Niccolò dei Greci
(Chiesa Greca)

17 Chiesa del Rosario
18 Chiesa di San Giovanni di Dio
19 Chiesa di San Giovanni Evang.
20 Chiesa di San Marco
21 Chiesa di San Matteo
22 Chiesa di Sant'Angelo
(Santa Maria di Costantinopoli)
23 Chiesa di Sant'Anna
24 Chiesa di Sant'Antonio da Padova
(San Giuseppe)
25 Chiesa di Sant'Irene (Teatini)
26 Chiesa di Santa Chiara
27 Chiesa di Santa Croce
e Palazzo dei Celestini
28 Chiesa di Santa Maria degli Angeli
(San Francesco di Paola)
29 Chiesa di Santa Maria del Carmine
30 Chiesa di Santa Maria della Luce
31 Chiesa di S. Maria della Porta
(San Luigi)
32 Chiesa di Santa Maria delle Grazie

33 Chiesa di Santa Teresa
34 Colonna e Statua di Sant'Oronzo
35 Conservatorio di Sant'Anna
36 Episcopio
37 Fontana dell'Armonia
38 Obelisco di Ferdinando I
39 Ospedale dello Spirito Santo (ex)
40 Piazza S. Oronzo
41 Porta Napoli
42 Porta Rudiae
43 Porta San Biagio
44 Pozzetto
45 Propilei P.zza Duomo
46 Sedile
47 Seminario
48 Teatro Comunale Paisiello
49 Teatro Romano
50 Teatro Politeama Greco
51 Villa Comunale
52 Villa Indraccolo
53 Villa Bray

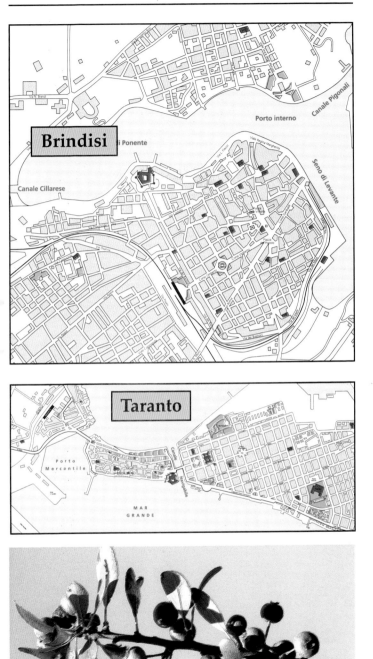

Index

2 Wonderful Apulia
3 All surrounded with the sea
8 The Cathedrals
16 The Castles
18 Castel del Monte
as it is described by two foreign travellers:
Janet Ross and Ferdinand Gregorovius

30 Brindisi and Gallipoli
in *Kitab-i bahriye* by Piri Re'is

34 The towers
37 The prehistory
the dinosaurs as the first inhabitants
44 An open museum
52 A Regione of Believers
with great sanctuaries and rupestrian churches

54 The *college* of san Nicola di Casole

65 The baroque
68 Martina Franca: a different town
70 The landscape

76 The long grassy paths
when millions of sheep went down from Abruzzo
80 Castellana Grotte
81 The Tremiti islands

82 Under the "trulli" of Alberobello
88 The east once again